Lucia - The Crowd Puller

An Investor's Journey

Thanai Kumar

This book is dedicated to my family. I thought of listing my family members separately then I had to worry about who I would thank first. Would it be my mom or wife, daughter or son, brother, or dad? You see the problem. So, I leave it at "family". Also dedicated to my friends who would be buying this book due to sheer pressure.

Table of Contents

Introduction

Congratulations on purchasing this book! This book is about the journey I as an investor had during the making of a Kannada movie. This movie was crowdfunded and I was one among the crowd. This book takes you through why, what, and how it all happened. If crowdsourcing and social media interest you then you must read ahead to learn about how both these concepts were used to bring about a change in the way movies are made and brought out to the general public. You will also get to enjoy a sprinkling of personal anecdotes.

Chapter Zero – Prologue

Lights, Camera, Action. Three words that a movie director yearns to say every day. They are the quintessential triggers in bringing a movie into the world. A director makes a movie because he has a story to tell. Cinema is the art-form he chooses to narrate the tale so that he can infuse his perceptions and emotions into the tale visually.

Lucia is a movie that was made entirely with the funds provided by the audience who wanted to watch brilliant cinema. The audience were common folk, who were given an option to choose the kind of movie they wanted to see. Movies being made were glorifying violence, sleaze on the pretext that it was what the audience wanted to watch. Lucia proved this wrong and started a new wave in the Kannada Film Industry. A new wave and a new hope which could result in pride being restored in the industry and bringing audiences back to the cinema halls. The hallowed box office is where a movie is declared a success.

Lucia did its 100 days run in Bangalore. The 100th show brought together all the people who made it possible to Cinepolis to watch it one last time in its 70mm glory. Emotions abounded at the close of the project. A project that had become the life-blood and passion for many over the past two years. You might be wondering what Lucia was and how it came to be? I present the story in this book.

The movie itself has two story threads running in parallel. One thread was shot in colour and another one in black and white. The director used the medium of colour very well to differentiate and tell us a story. I feel that if it had been a play or a book it would have been very difficult to piece it together. Cinematic liberties were evoked to make it work in the movie.

Pawan Kumar is the Writer-Director of the movie. Pawan, a college dropout wanted to do something different from the run-of-the-mill movie which had a gun-wielding goon chasing the heroine. He wanted to attract a broad diaspora of audience and without under-estimating their sensibilities keep them engaged to figure out what happens next. He had no professional training in movie making but he was passionate about this story. He reached out to a few producers in the industry and when they did not agree to finance it without making changes to commercialize it, Pawan reached out to the audience to help him make this movie and the rest is history.

Pawan had three successful movies before Lucia out of which he was credited for Story and Screenplay in two and was the Writer-Director for one. Still, he had to reach out to the crowd to fund his movie. How did that happen? Why would producers not want to fund movies like Lucia? This is mainly because of audience segmentation. Film producers want to make movies that can bring back money to them. They segment audience demographic based on different cities, towns, and villages that the movie releases in. The movies are also categorized loosely based on mass-appeal or class-appeal, multiplex, or single-screen theatres. The number of multiplex audience is considerably lesser than the single-screen theatre audience. The producers believed that the story of Lucia would resonate with the audiences in cities and bigger towns and therefore would run only in multiplexes. Kannada movies only had a pan Karnataka release and so they did not want to take a chance on returns. Also, there was no big star backing the project. This meant that the first day collections were further reduced. Most Kannada movies banked on the star power and the fan associations to bring in the crowds in the first week where the producers made the most money. To complicate matters, Lucia did not have the usual commercial elements which could drive collections. This left Pawan with little choice but to do what no one expected him to do. He went straight to the audience and let them decide if such a movie had to be made. He would be very surprised on how the audience responded.

What are the two important elements in making a movie? A story and the corresponding audience. Now the story and the maker were in place and only the audience had to come together to fund it. Pawan united the audience in a way that was never done before in the Kannada or Indian Film scene. Karnataka has a population of close to 6 Crores (60 million) out of which roughly 1-3% watch Kannada movies in a theatre. This number becomes even smaller if there is no well-known star. Therefore, there is a trade-off when movies are made to not accommodate the likes of a considerable chunk of the viewing public, in order to get the maximum number of people to watch it in a theatre. This chunk of viewers resort to watching movies in other languages or make do with other forms of entertainment. This was the audience Pawan tried to reach out to who would support his movie and watch it. Thus, the concept of "Audience Films" was formulated. Pawan had a website called "Hometalkies" which was an OTT platform for Kannada movies even before the likes of Amazon Prime Video and Netflix became popular in India. He re-purposed this platform to create a stage for good movie ideas. The Audience would choose a good movie before the movie was made and provide their backing for it. This would help budding filmmakers to go ahead and make their movie without having to worry about the commercial aspects as the microfinance provided by the audience would fund the movie. That is how Lucia was made and it saw a theatrical release on the 6th of Sep 2013.

Lucia, the movie was about Lucid Dreaming. The protagonist indulges in lucid dreaming and what he experiences forms the crux of the movie. It has the elements of a love story. The protagonist was played by Sathish Ninasam. He was ably supported by Sruthi Hariharan as the lead actress in the movie. Achyuth Kumar played a very good supporting character in the movie. The movie also has now acclaimed actor-director Rishab Shetty as a cop in a small role. The entire movie was shot in 65 days. The cast and crew had to work hard on a tough schedule to get the final product out. The end product Lucia with a total running time of 138.26 minutes is there for everyone to watch. Lucia, a mainstream movie being crowdsourced in Kannada for the very first time, launched the careers of many artists in the industry. The Assistant Director of the movie was hired using a promo test online. Candidates were required to make a short film about what they thought Lucia was and had to upload that to YouTube. The Music Director for the movie, Poornachandra Tejaswi was working in the Technology Industry. He quit his regular day job and joined Pawan to work on Lucia. The first song of the movie went viral, garnering 1 lakh views in the first three weeks from across the globe. Once the movie was out it got accolades from established industry big-wigs

Irrfan Khan put out a video on YouTube and said, "I saw the film and I am quite impressed with it. It has a very interesting plot and has earnest performances by the lead actors".

Anurag Kashyap tweeted, "Go see 'Lucia' a brave, fearless new Kannada film. Thoroughly entertaining".

It also entered the Oscar race to represent India in the foreign film language category. The current IMDB rating for Lucia is 8.3. Compiling the data after the theatrical run, 77% of its viewers came from Bangalore and 23% outside of Bangalore. Multiplex accounted for 67% of earnings and single-screen cinemas 33%. When you want something from all your heart the entire universe conspires to make it happen (dialogue borrowed from a popular Hindi movie).

Chapter One – 70 mm Investment

"Naanu agiyuvalli kallu, ajja agiyuvalli mannu" – Kannada Proverb

"Where I dig I hit stones, where grandfather digs its soft soil"

"Baanigondu Elle Ellidhe..Ninnasaegelli kone idhe.."

("Sky is limitless and so are your desires")

My daughter was singing this happily in the adjacent room, while I sat in front of my laptop with my finger poised to click on "Invest Now". This song alludes to eternal words on celluloid etched in the minds of movie-goers across generations. My daughter had learned it from my father who is a huge fan of the 1970s Kannada movies. Growing up, movies was one of the unifiers in my family of diverse opinions.

Cinema is poetry in motion. It can engulf you, swallow you, make you, or break you. It transports you to a world where you could time travel at the cost of two liters of petrol. Movies, in India, are a legitimate reason to spend time and money across economic and social strata. On the streets of Indian metro cities, you may be walking, stealing, or relieving yourself and in all probability, there will be a huge hoarding of a movie star at a stone's throw away staring at you.

"Movie? Are you sure?" is a question I have been asked many times in my life, mostly when I suggest squandering away time by watching a movie when there are other pressing deadlines in life like an exam the next day. But this time it was Siri asking me and for a reason, you cannot quite guess! On the one hand, I could not lie to her, and on the other, I wanted to sound confident. I began by telling her that it was a science fiction movie being made in Kannada. "Forget your money, only love stories make money in India", she said. I had very little data to prove otherwise. I was not sure if this movie had a romantic angle at all let alone being a love story. It did not help that the proposed title of the movie was not only super short but it did not mean anything in the languages I knew.

Decision making is either spontaneous or carefully planned. One follows intuition and past experiences and the other follows data-driven insight. In this case, I had very little information about this movie and I felt that it was easiest to make a decision then. I could just toss a coin and take the plunge. God knows what I was thinking but God alone knows what I was thinking!

Humans make snap decisions many times in life. The most visible thin-slicing decision I had taken was to get married. Would lending money for a movie become the most notorious decision I would take? Whenever we need to take decisions, we look for inspiration from the immediate life surrounding us. We look for a sign that tells you to "go live your life". Around this time, a close friend of mine bought his dream bike, the Enfield Bullet bike for 1.5 Lakh Rupees. He felt like a king cruising around on it with arms and legs expansively encircling the bike. But very soon, most owners of such bikes realize that when they drive on the crowded city roads, they are never going to be granted the space that maneuvering this motorbike demands. A BMTC public bus charging down the road always gets more respect and space on Bangalore's relentless roads compared to any other means of transport. In the case of my friend, common sense prevailed and he parked his Bullet and purchased a big hulk of an SUV. This was not the best sign.

When you grow up in a middle-class family, the biggest lesson you are taught is to not take risks. If it involves money being invested in anything other than the tried and trusted, then you should go to the temple, pray to God and forget that you even had the idea. For otherwise, what would people say! I thought about family reactions. "What will my father-in-law think?" I asked myself. As you may have rightly observed, I was not worried about what my father or mother would think. I was worried about what my father-in-law would think? All the married men reading my book would understand why I put the father in law before anyone else. I am sure the creators of the millennial term "bae" weren't thinking of the plight of married men! I went a step ahead and played the conversation in my head since I was sure I had to be prepared to answer a few questions.

"Hello Uncle, I plan to invest in a movie. It's a Kannada movie and I think it will be a good investment".

My father-in-law assuming the role of my auditor hammers me with "What is the return on investment? Will you get more than the interest offered by NSC? What is the guarantee that the movie will make money? What if it becomes a loss? Who will refund the money if it's a loss? Are there are any guarantors for the movie? Are you going to quit your job now that you will become a Producer? Will you sit at home and eat with what my daughter is going to earn?"

At a loss for words, I start perspiring.

I shifted my thoughts to what my mother-in-law might ask me. Thankfully not many questions came to my head, but I did visualize her giving me an anxious smile. For now, I was determined to take it as a good sign.

However, I had still not given a convincing answer to Siri's question and I did not have one. They say one should draw upon life lessons for showing the way. One of my managers once told me to not run behind money and that money would come running to you. This was a response I got when I had asked why my salary raise was so negligible. I did take his advice seriously and stopped chasing money but money also stopped chasing me. I was not better off in either way. But I decided to test this ideology again in a different context and see if it worked. I stopped looking for a reason why I wanted to lend money to this grandiose scheme and waited for the answer to appear in my Facebook message. None arrived other than a request to plough some land in Farmville. So, my advice to everyone is to never stop chasing what you want in life.

An investment is an asset purchased with the idea that the asset will provide income in the future or will later be sold at a higher price for a profit. I did not have a great track record of investing in the right places. I would generally look at investments as something that could earn me money in the short term. It had never really worked for me according to my definition of future or profit. It was almost like a black cloud followed me everywhere I invested. A popular bank was doing very well and they decided to go public. The Initial Public Offering was made and there was a massive advertisement drive to grab eyeballs. But I held firm and did not invest. I guess I was trying to crack the equation where the PE ratio was the left-hand side and the Da Vinci Code was the right-hand side! The stock was listed and boom the price went up. It had to, as I had still not bought a single stock. It kept moving up and reached a point that seemed like it was the highest ever it would get. I still did not enter the market at that price. It went up further and experts believed the stock price could go higher. I now waited like a crouching tiger. One crash was what I was waiting for and it came soon. The stock tanked and that is when I pounced, I mean bought the stock. It tanked further and showed no signs of improvement. Did I make the mistake again of buying too soon? I hoped not and I waited patiently. There was a recovery and it soon passed the price that I had bought it at. The next morning it went up a little further and stayed there. Just as a kid who has sown a seed, checks every hour to see if the shoot came up, I would go check the price almost every day hoping for a miracle. It never happened. Patience is a virtue which the virtuous have. I was not one of them. I had had enough and I decided to sell the shares of that bank around noon. It was not as if I needed the money but I could not bear the thought of the stock tanking again. I placed the sell order, closed the browser, and got back to work. The next morning the cute CNBC reporter happily reported about how well the stock did in the last two trading sessions of the day. The stock had zoomed to be the top grosser and had broken all previous records. My sale had happened just before that. I managed a wry smile at my luck and focused on how cute the anchor was. That day it was evident to me why they hired her.

"You are getting carried away, but I do trust your decision," Siri told me with the same confidence as an eleventh batsman facing a fast bowler. It was a very complex and loaded statement if I could say so myself. I was definitely getting carried away. What I haven't told you so far is that we were living in Kansas at that time and it's easy to get carried away as it's the land of Wizard of Oz! I was doing my best to sell the idea that if the movie made profits, we would make some more money back. "Enter only if you have full faith and trust" was the line, from the blog about the movie, that was jumping out at me. A line like that will lead you to believe that it was some get-rich-quick scheme which promised to double your money in no time. My beloved wife was trying to bring to my attention that this could be one of those. There was no guarantee or assurance other than the fact that this was from a director who had directed a movie earlier.

With my track record on investments, I could not hope for anything earth-shattering. My core competency was nothing remotely related to the movies. I had strong experience as a viewer and that was all I knew about movies. I knew that making a movie cost a lot and I wouldn't make one ever in my life. But here I was transferring money, on the click-easy online banking site, to the maker of Lucia.

Chapter Two: Social Media

"Kuri kobbidashtu kurubanige laabaa" – Kannada Proverb

"The fatter the goat the better for the butcher"

Kansas was a happy phase for my family. We had a lot of firsts to attribute to this phase. Also, a second, my second kid was born there. The public libraries in the United States typically do not have a limit to the number of materials that one could borrow from them. Siri and I would have been one of the very few members who have probably viewed half their movie collection. Every night was a movie night! We became addicted to good movies. We had watched so many movies that when we moved back to India and subscribed to Netflix and Amazon Prime video, there were not many movies left to watch other than the latest ones (in a few languages). We not only watched movies we borrowed from the library but also on streaming platforms. The technologist in me became adept at setting up and connecting various gadgets to the TV to be able to maximize movie watching pleasure.

I believe man is an anti-social animal. Social media has given him the right tools to sit safely in isolation behind his computer and profess how social he is. One such popular social platform was where I discovered hometalkies.com. It was a movie portal for viewing Kannada movies online legally by renting it for a limited time.

The journey brought forth in this book all began one evening after watching a Kannada movie called "Sidlingu" on hometalkies.com, I noticed a tiny link at the corner of the website in a different color which stood out from the rest of the site. The link was titled "Lucia" and before my brain could process what was happening my finger got trigger-happy and had clicked on that link.

"What strikes the head depends on what the mouse clicked."

I spent a lot of time reading the content available on the site. As I repeatedly read through, I was convinced that I was on the brink of something big. It was the call to buy tickets to a Kannada movie that was not yet made. No information was provided about the movie, story, cast or plot. It was a detailed blog from the director about why he was approaching the audience and asking them to buy the tickets to a movie he was yet to make. The director gave the reader two options. The first option was to buy tickets to the movie at a cost of $25 each. The second option was to be a part of the venture by lending money to make the movie. Now, how many times have you bought a movie ticket without knowing anything about it let alone help to make the movie? The only known entity was the director of the movie. This situation had to be analyzed a little more deeply.

Problem statement – Should I buy a ticket or should I invest and increase risk?

Mathematically, a movie with characteristic set C needs to overcome a set of N(C) risks to be successful. Considering P(r) is the probability of the risk occurring then I(r) which is the impact of risk reduces when the number of risks reduces. Meaning that (r1...r N(C)) where N(C) would be close to 1.

So, if the movie is made then the amount of risk when released would be

$$R(C) = \sum_{i=1}^{N(C)} P(r_i, C) * I(r_i, C)$$

.

To reduce the risk, the characteristic set had to be explored. This is what I deduced

Unknown entities

Hero = x

Heroine = y

Villain = z

Plot = α

Lucia – The Crowd Puller

Release Date = β

Music Director or Singers = Ω

Known Entities-:

Director = Pawan Kumar

Budget = 50 Lakhs INR

Given that the character set was uncharacteristically ambiguous, would the better idea be to buy a ticket worth $25 or contribute to the making and wait to see if there is profit or loss? I thought that with the number of variables in the equation, the best way to solve this conundrum was to evaluate the risk logically.

Returns on $25 = One time watching of a movie

Returns on contribution to make the movie = Credits in the movie + Blu-ray of the movie + Possible returns proportional to the contribution based on business

The biggest known entity was the director Pawan Kumar. I had the opportunity of watching a few of his movies. Although as a director there was only one movie called "Lifeu Ishtene", there were a few others where Pawan was involved technically and in a few movies even as an actor. Pawan had written the story and screenplay for two movies before this one, 'Manasaare' and 'Pancharangi'. Most of his work was appreciated and well received by the audience. This gave me some more attributes to make a decision. All of these attributes are not directly tangible but if one takes a closer look at what is at stake, a pattern then emerges.

In my opinion, success has many measurements and is extremely personal. One could choose to survive in any industry by doing work that was just enough. As one of my managers never tired of telling me "Meets expectations is a good rating." It was mostly not because of what I did or did not do but because he wanted to have a nice-looking performance assessment bell curve. When you do what is expected and continue to maintain status-quo, you are happy, your parents are happy, your father-in-law is happy, your relatives are happy and your dog at home is anyway happy. Once in a while, there comes along a person who does what no one expects him to do and creates a paradigm shift. But on the bell curve, it would be difficult to say whether he would be assessed as outstanding because that would depend on the success measurement used.

In the case of "Lucia", the product was the script which was known only to him. A movie is a director's medium. Pawan would have the ultimate control of the result. If the movie was well-received, he would have the opportunity to give his career a new direction and a new meaning. If the movie became successful, he would be the person who would gain the most. And since it was a movie with multiple contributors, the biggest risk-taker was also Pawan himself. He had everything at stake with Lucia. If the movie failed, he would have to work hard and get back to being the mediocre person in his industry. There was no guarantee he would be welcome again to do that mediocre job. At times like this, questions give answers and unknown entities stand resolved. Would Pawan risk his career and chart a course to a dead-end I wondered. It did not matter to me anymore if there were more unknown entities. I wanted to know what options were available to invest.

I decided to go ahead and contribute money to make the movie and so did many others with the fond hope that a great product would be delivered. Pawan's philosophical take was that even if the movie failed, we all had a great story to tell our grandchildren!

Despite all this excitement, there was one thing that I could not have foreseen in my wildest dreams. Why the movie was called "Lucia". It was not appealing. It felt like the name of a flop movie already. Even before it was made it had the characteristic of being a dud. Shakespeare said, "What 's in a name"? And named his book "As you like it". Ask me and I will tell you what is in a name. Every first introduction results in the other person contorting my name. After trying for many years to get the correct pitch, tone, clarity, and bass required to convey my name so that it is immediately understood, I have given up and let people assume whatever they feel like. One contortion of my name that has topped the probability list is "Chennai."

14

Name, they say is the identity of a person, but whoever said this did not realize that the name is given to the person by his parents. So how does this become his "identity"? I am sure given a chance 'Calvin', from Calvin and Hobbes, would have chosen his name as 'Dynamite David'!

A friend of mine told me about his uncle naming his kid Freeshow for no apparent reason. He wanted to call him Frisho but he spelt it all wrong.

Let's view this problem from the parents' perspective. There is a lot of pressure that parents feel when naming their children. In our case, we also had the global experience in mispronunciation of our names. When we were blessed with a daughter, Siri, and I decided to give her a name that is not tough to pronounce and has a good sound to it. One more criterion for the name was that it should have the "correct" meaning. My name means "son" in my native tongue and my wife calls me by this name! Don't get me wrong, I like my name. But we wanted to ensure that we gave her a name that is not complicated but still unique and nice which was a big responsibility on our shoulders.

Having established the facts and after a lot of research, we named our daughter "Vihitha". We both loved the name as soon as we heard it. The meaning of Vihitha is appropriate (in Sanskrit). We tried to see if the name can be tweaked in various ways to be sure that nothing negative comes out of the name. Having done all that we went ahead and named her in an elaborate ritual.

In one social gathering, a few friends of mine asked what we had named our daughter. I told all of them her name is Vihitha and went on to tell that it meant appropriate.

In one social gathering, a few friends of mine asked what we had named our daughter. I told all of them that her name is Vihitha and went on to tell that it meant appropriate.

"Oh, so she will be Miss Appropriate (misappropriate)?" was the reply from one smart friend.

Chapter Three: The Plunge

"Kaasiddare Kailasa" – Kannada Proverb

"Heaven's door opens for one who has money"

"What do you think the story will be like?" asked Siri and I replied, "A science fiction movie which no producer wanted to produce sounds like it's going to be an interesting idea". Sarcasm apart the thought that this was something no established producer wanted to fund started to pick my curiosity. The fact remained that no one wanted to listen to the story. They rejected it outright as they did not have the time or did not want to do creative work. The fact that it was a unique story was comforting to me. We already trusted the director enough to help him make the movie so I had no second thoughts on the story. But I still held on to the doubts on how it would be received. Only time would tell.

In our industry and by 'our' industry I mean the industry that enabled me to contribute money to a movie, the tech industry or the IT industry, the biggest problem which remains unsolved to date is how to evaluate the performance of an individual. There is no sure-shot successful method. In that case, maybe the whole idea of evaluation is fundamentally wrong and needs to be corrected. The outcome of such an evaluation is rewards and recognition. Rewards are something that can put a dent to the shareholder value so recognition is something that happens more often compared to rewards.

I will present a fictitious account of how recognition is decided. Two managers met for an hour on a Friday afternoon. "How about recognizing Avinash?" asked one manager. "Oh, but what he does is routine stuff. His project did not have any issues. So, it must be easy to be Avinash", the other replied. "Then how about Karthik? He spends a lot of time at the office, must be very hardworking" asked the first manager. The second manager drummed his fingers on the table for half a minute and said "He may have a gap in skills which could be the reason why he is spending so much time in office". After Karthik was relegated to the realms of mediocrity the managers kept on the hunt to find the right one to recognize. "I think we should consider Mahesh. He has been getting accolades at the client site and has been an inspiration to many" said the first manager. The second manager was enraged "Who? Mahesh? He is earning a handsome salary sitting in the United States. There is no need to recognize him. What with the Rupee falling against the Dollar, he must be saving a lot?" By now the two managers had finished their cup of tea and were at risk of having to set up another meeting to make the decision. That is when they hit upon a brilliant idea. The second manager asked excitedly "How about Rohith?" "Oh, I forgot about him. I am not sure what he does. Do you know what he is doing? Do you understand his work?" asked the other. "No, his work is always a mystery to me. Must be something complicated". Happy at the prospect of a decision the first manager says "Yes, I agree. I too find it hard to get to the root of his work. So, it must be something exemplary. Why don't we recognize him? We can use the word 'Exemplary' on the certificate too". While Rohith was busy updating his status on a social networking platform, he receives the memo that he has been recognized as the employee of the month.

I was worried about a similar fate for a good movie. Either a committee would be formed who would not understand the movie so give it an award and then the movie had to bear the brunt of being an "Award Movie" or the public would fail to recognize the movie as it did not have any stars among the cast. During my childhood, movies which had subtitles were always a taboo. Subtitles were mostly for movies which would be telecast pan India on Sundays. But an entire generation of movie watchers held an unconscious bias against attempting to understand such movies. The fact that the director of Lucia always wanted to subtitle it, made me worried about how this would be perceived by the current generation.

A movie with a star cast in it was assured to get a good opening response due to the brand value carried by the star, irrespective of the content. Our movie lacked such big names. Would that impact the success of this project? I had moved on to my next set of questions which of course had very few answers.

History was being made and at the same time, one has to look back into history to see if this was that unique. Folklore has it that a guy would carry a drum into the villages and beat the drum in the village square shouting "Kelrappo Kelri". The sound of the drum would indicate an important announcement. The King would use this messenger service to bring awareness or to project a problem whose solution he needed from the people. The village folk would stop in their tracks to assemble and listen to the drummer's announcement. Drawing a parlance, Lucia was a similar exercise. Pawan was using the internet as his drummer and he drummed information into many folks who were reading his blog posts. He posed the question of making a movie in hostile conditions and challenged everyone on the world wide web to be a rebel with a cause. People criticized his move of going public asking for funds. But that would not stop Pawan, the artist.

The appeal for investment had resulted in a record-breaking response. The target movie budget was Rs.50,00000. In the first three days after the option to purchase tickets or invest in the movie was made public, Rs.22,50,000 had been collected. In about 20 odd days they had collected close to Rs.40,00000. I believe such a response was possible because of the range of options provided for the buyers of the movie tickets. They could purchase a ticket to a yet-to-be-made movie at a cost of Rs.1250 or Rs.5000. Each option came with its benefits. There was another option to invest bigger amounts in the project and become an investor. The director was planning to close the investment option in a couple of days, such was the response. This was a record collection for a script that had no conventional takers. Not one of the investors had read the script but they all believed in the movement. The magic number of Rs.50,00000 was collected in 27 days. A total of 110 people had contributed various amounts to reach this magical number. On the last day, two transfers happened at the same time taking the total money collected to 51 lakhs. I was secretly ecstatic that others were, either foolish or brave, like me to lend more money.

On March 12th, 2012, I decided to fund the money in my limited capacity. Personally, it was a big moment for us. Investing in movies was unheard of in my family and this would be perceived as being similar to gambling, betting on a horse race, etc. If my parents knew about it, I was sure I wouldn't have been allowed to do this. Being away from home and in the US at that time helped. They didn't give it too much thought when I informed them about it casually.

Now that money had been procured, a movie had to be made. Or would the director just pack his bags, move to an undisclosed location, and change his identity? I imagined what would happen in the event of Pawan running away with all the money. I would first have to call my father-in-law.

"Hello uncle, that movie thing I was talking about like you said was a really bad idea. I don't think there is a future in the movie industry." My father-in-law would have chimed in *"Yes my son, what did I tell you? I knew that these days youngsters like you know nothing about financial management. Whoever thought to invest in a movie is a good idea? Ridiculous!"*

Thankfully I had mitigated this risk, I hadn't told anyone apart from Siri about this venture yet.

They say success has a lot of fathers and failure is an orphan. But in a crowdsourced venture, both success and failure are equally shared. It is always directly proportional to the equity. I as an investor was prepared to see either side of this coin. But somewhere deep inside I was sure of the model and its success. We were all a part of Team Lucia. At this juncture, a mail landed into my inbox from Pawan.

"Lucia is a fictional story. It will just be a 2-hour movie. It's not about a great person or an issue. It will not change the world. But the process of making it will give hope to a lot of people and hence could play a small role in changing their lives...".

There was a subtle hint from the maker. Up until this email, Pawan used to sign his emails with his standard signature "Pawan Kumar -

www.pawantheactor.com . This changed soon after the money was collected. The mail indicating that the funding for the movie was complete and we were all set to kick start the project had his signature as "Pawan Kumar - Director for Lucia". I read the mail and slept well that night.

Pawan kept us updated about the plans and progress of the movie. Ideas poured in from most investors regarding how to market this product and what could be done to achieve the wow factor. A lot of ideas were generated about providing better marketing channels, better online presence, legal help to ensure we got maximum coverage, Lucia T-shirts, selling the premiere tickets uniquely, and so on. In their enthusiasm, the crowd (funding contributors) had inadvertently provided the raw material to what could be the base of future actions.

I have spoken about the reverse Midas Touch I had with investments. Any stock I buy has to fall, resulting in buyer's remorse and any stock I sell immediately goes up in price after I sell. This has been such an invariable pattern that I could have become a stock consultant and made money in that way at least. I didn't know how this would pan out with the investment in Lucia. I would find out very soon.

We got a mail telling us that Diganth was going to be the lead actor in the movie. Him being a rising star in the industry, I was thrilled that we had roped him in. This would drive the commercials home and my father in law will not have a chance to question me. But not everything is straight forward, is it? Soon after I had transferred the money, we received an email from Pawan that Diganth was not able to provide enough time for Lucia and hence mutually it was agreed that he could not be the hero of the movie. So, we were back to square one with no lead actor. The newspapers spoke about how some stars were busy and had no time for Lucia. As a person whose money was making the movie, I believed that it should have a popular face in the lead. That way there would be the assurance that on the opening day there would be a crowd waiting to watch the movie.

There was a fine balancing act required between making the movie artsy and commercial and Pawan called it 'a tight rope walk'. He and the cinematographer had taken a decision to use a basic Canon EOS 5D Camera which is a digital SLR that can also shoot video. This was a different choice compared to the usual movie cameras. The team was willing to try new things on the technical aspects to keep the cost low while not lowering the quality. Pawan believed that it was the story, performances, and quality of the result that had to be top-notch. He believed that a great honest performance by an actor shot on a decent camera was more rewarding than having the best camera with an actor who couldn't play the character. The team was considering Sathish Ninasam to play the lead. Even before Pawan finalized it, the newspapers ran a story that he was the hero. That was it, our movie had got its lead actor.

Then came the next best news from Pawan, well at least in my perspective. He was looking for a leading lady for the movie. For me, this meant that there would be a romantic angle. I happily called out to Siri "It's time for some Jamma Jamma Jamma Jammaja."

Chapter Four: Star Material?

"Chinte illadavanige santheyallu niddhe" – Kannada Proverb

"The one who has no worries can sleep even in a crowded fair"

Everyone grows up with impossible dreams which seem so possible depending on how close in age you are to 5. I have dreamt of being a movie director, story writer, and even a spot boy. But I never dreamt that I would be funding a movie! But magical things happen in the journey of life!

One thing we noticed while living in the US is that people who are far away from their homelands are somehow more connected to their roots. They find reasons and avenues to be closer to India and its culture. My family was part of a cultural not for profit organization called the 'Chandana Kannada Sangha' which is a Kannada cultural group based in Kansas state in the US. The group plans and executes several cultural events throughout the year. We were lucky to attend one such event where a popular Kannada theater group presented a play. The host brought me over to introduce me to the cast of the play. In order that this confession does not cause real damage to my marital status, I would like to clarify that I have always tried hard to strike up a conversation with the ladies. I would ensure that it was usually something funny, something that would interest them and in turn make me look good. Here I was, about to meet a budding, young, good-looking actor. What do you think I spoke about? Yes, you guessed it right my intelligent readers. I had an instant conversation starter, the best first line I could ever say to a girl like that. Such moments do not come often in one's life and it was right there for the taking. I went up and introduced myself and there was an immediate connection by talking about Lucia and how they were looking for a female lead. She was happy to hear that and wanted me to talk to her dad! That fall of events doesn't happen too often I admit. Her father was a popular comedy actor and was extremely happy to hear that I would be able to help. Knowing that he has been in the Kannada movie industry for decades I wondered why he would need my help. He must have been humouring me since he was a comedian. For once I didn't care, it was nice to get into the good books of this aspiring actor and become one of her friends on social media. Moreover, I could do all this under the supervision of my better half. So, my marital bliss was intact.

I saw an opportunity to make a special contribution to the movie by finding its female lead. I sent across my reference for the leading lady role to the director. I wrote to him in detail about her lineage, her performance and her positive attitude. Maybe lady luck did not shine on me that day because I never heard back on this subject from the director. I was disappointed but had to convince myself that this perhaps was because of the movie maker's principles against nepotism. I also gave myself a real reason that the leading lady had already been signed and therefore no interest was shown towards my reference.

The IT industry is a place where diversity and inclusion are deemed very important. As a manager, I have always valued a diverse opinion. Most companies have diversity champions to help increase the focus on diversity in their organization. It is a pity that most of such champions are women! There is a misconception that diversity champions have to be a female leader! I believe it defies the purpose. In a movie, there is no such bias. If there is a female role one needs to hire an actress. The rules are clear. Unless the movie has Kamal Hassan. He can star in any role, no gender bias.

Like the IT industry, the Kannada film industry also needs a focused effort for diversity and inclusion. Out of the two hundred and fifty applications that had come for auditions, there was a total of 3 women candidates. A mere 1.2% of the applicants were female although there were vacancies in leading actors of both genders. Was this because girls do not think this is an honorable profession? Or was it because they did not believe in this movie?

We got an email that the shoot for the movie was going to begin. There would be a press release on 14th May to announce the movie and 21st May would be the first day of the shoot. To me, this summed up to all the main actors being finalized and the script was ready!

A few days before the actual Press Meet for the movie the director arranged a virtual hang out session where multiple folks joined the same event. It was a "Successful Experiment". We could all take part in the session with little difficulty. Having tested this platform all of the investors were quite excited to be a part of the actual press meet that was slated to happen.

The Lucia technical team had made huge plans for a Press Meet. A gala event which was to be showcased to all the investors from various countries. All the emails were sent out and teams were ready to see their investments being put to use and the movie being announced. The entire cast and crew of Lucia were present at the event. Yogaraj Bhat, Vijay Prasad, and Manjunath (producer of Lifeu Ishtene) were some of the dignitaries present at the meet. They did have some kind words for the project and also spoke in its favor. The investors were all eager to watch the event live. Poor folks, they all had forgotten there was a guy known as Murphy who had predicted that anything that can go wrong will go wrong and usually at the worst time! The media had assembled in a hall which was on the lower floors of the hotel building. The hotel manager informed the director that their internet signals did not reach the party hall and that there was no way they could provide the internet to the hall. The location of the room was such that no amount of wireless data cards could provide the required data connectivity. Everything was set for the event and the event had to go on. The live online telecast of the press release had to be shelved. Technology not helping a platform that had been technically funded! 2g, 3g, 4g, nim ajji, had to make do with a recorded event played back later.

In a press meet the journalists always ask intelligent questions. The panel had to be on top of their game to get things right. The Lucia team also made some T-shirts to popularize the movie and bring awareness about the brand. The lead actor and the director were sporting these t-shirts for the press event and this was something one of the journalists noticed. He wanted to know why it was just the lead actor and the director wearing the "Lucia" branded t-shirt and not the entire team. Was there any mutiny in the ranks? The Lucia team was quick to defend and convince the journalist that there were better ways to spend the money collected for the movie other than printing and wearing t-shirts.

We got to learn that Sruthi Hariharan was going to be the lead actress in the movie. She was a Malayalee by birth but could speak Kannada like so many other Malayalees in Bangalore. If there is one community that blends well with any culture it is the Malayalees. They are everywhere imaginable. The popular joke is that they all work very hard once they leave Kerala and hence you will find them all over the world. My connection with Malayalees goes a long way. I was at one of my friend's house who happens to be a Malayalee. His grandmother from Kerala was visiting Bangalore. We were a gang of 6 guys who were at his house. Almost all were Malayalees apart from me. His grandmother was very sure that I was the only Malayalee in the gathering! I am not sure why but that profile seems to fit me well. Most people assume that I am a Malayalee. Could it be my moustache? Laletta Zindabad!

Sruthi was rejected after her first audition but something about her made Pawan give her a second chance. The movie shoot continued and we got regular updates on the progress. Thanks to the meticulous planning in the script stage the shoot time was reduced to a bare minimum number of days. This helped keep the budget in check.

The news anchor on TV was talking about how Pawan, the actor, had collected a huge sum of money from gullible audiences across the world and promised to make an audience funded movie. The idea was novel according to the news anchor but the execution wasn't. He had managed to transfer all of the money to an unknown account in Switzerland and had made good. I was very worried about why all of this was happening. I had nowhere to hide and was expecting the phone to ring any minute now and my father in law demanding how I was going to take care of his daughter, my wife! Thankfully no phone call came but the alarm rang and woke me up from my slumber. There was no scam and Pawan was very much around. While I was having a nightmare, an email from Pawan landed in my inbox.

The mail said that close to half the movie shoot had been completed. I could not believe it. The mail had a lot of other details but all that was a haze to me. Everything else seemed immaterial and all I could think of was that we were making the first crowdsourced movie in Kannada. It was my first investment in a movie! It was time to party. After the euphoria amped down, I read the mail in its entirety and there was news for me.

Chapter Five: Strength of the Crowd

"Ganji kudiyuvanige meese hidiyuvavanobba" – Kannada Proverb

"An assistant to hold up the moustache for the person drinking soup"

Lucia on completion would be the first crowdfunded Kannada movie. Aside from this credit, other factors became a study in crowdsourcing.

A picture is worth a thousand words as all of us know. If you have any doubts about this, please take out your PAN card or the Voter's ID card and take a look at that photo. I have heard this many times in my life especially after I have shown people my passport size photograph. Not sure what it is in passport-sized photos, it brings the "best" in all of us. Costume and locations are very critical to a movie's character. In a movie, with a strict budget, the makers develop a special antenna for conveying more with less. Pawan, the director, had prior experience in the movie "Lifeu Ishtene" where he wanted the opening scene to be at an airport. The easiest option was to film the scene at a film studio with an inbuilt airport set but that would be expensive. Filming at an actual airport is chaotic, very expensive, and time-taking with permissions, crowd control, etc. Instead of continuing the script with the airport, he changed it to a saloon and a junk yard. That helped keep the cost low and did not take anything away from the story. So as a writer, you can have the liberty to pen your thoughts any which way you want. The same when translated or transcribed into screenplay it has to change keeping in mind the various constraints a movie maker has to go through.

For Lucia, Pawan listed down 70 locations which were a requirement of the script and provided some details around them. He reached out to the people who had funded his movie to help him source such locations. The team rallied around him and provided locations in a way that brought down the cost of the movie. Pawan modified the script based on the locations that were sourced, all the while keeping the sanctity of the script intact. There was a well-wisher who even loaned a Harley Davidson bike to help frame a song that required a sophisticated look. Kindness, ingenuity, and passion are at the heart of the movie Lucia.

Some scenes required a large number of people to be present in the frame. Pawan used a popular social media site to crowdsource the crowd! A few days before the shoot he would post information regarding filming a scene at a particular location and anyone interested in watching the shoot could come and be part of the scene itself. A lot of movie crazy folks like me wouldn't pass up such a chance to possibly be shown in a movie frame. It was a win-win situation.

In the IT industry, often a person quits a company, not because he is paid less but because of a lack of engagement. A people manager's job, therefore, is not enviable because the main job role is to keep his or her team engaged and working towards the organization's goals. This is exactly what one small campaign by Pawan achieved. The quest was to find the perfect T-Shirt. He created an online contest "Buy a T-Shirt, make a Movie" on a popular social media platform to get t-shirt ideas and a small inflow of funds. All the techies who followed Pawan on this platform were fueled by the ambition of being the designer of Lucia t-shirts. They submitted designs and also shared this with their connections. This created a buzz on social media. The link was shared, people spoke about it and were engaged with the brand Lucia. Then there was a masterstroke to further engagement. The best design would also be selected by the crowd of followers making it a democratic transparent process. The crowd decided which was the best design and the winner got to keep a share from the proceeds from the sale of the T-Shirt. The engagement that this campaign achieved, was exponentially larger than the money that the t-shirt sales had brought. The fact that the community was involved in designing the T-Shirt, submitting entries, asking others to submit their entries, and selecting the winner created a sense of belonging among a large number of people.

The name of Lucia's production company is Audience Films. In an audience film, it was not surprising at all that the audience was also crowdsourced! I must have piqued your curiosity enough to make you go watch the movie by now. That's one way. This solution was extrapolated and it proved effective. A whopping 110 people invested money to make a movie. These 110 people would tell at least 20 other people about this movie. This way they have created the first wave. The first wave of people would at least share this information with 10 other people. This kind of chain marketing helped in generating the hype and the word of mouth publicity helped Lucia. There was a demand to watch the movie already at a time when the Kannada film audience had stopped stepping into the theater to watch one. They would wait for it to be aired on television so that they could catch the movie. We were hoping things would be different with Lucia. Only time would tell.

For the people who started working in the IT industry in the 1990s or early 2000s, the office environment consisted of a cubicle whose walls were tall enough to see the top of your neighbor's head. In most cubicles, there would be an array of Gods guarding over the code and ensuring that it compiles in the first attempt. There would also be an occasional poster or calendar and a bouquet of yellow post-its. Taking breaks meant drinking a cup of Biju's chai and team meetings were held by huddling around one or two cubicles. The millennials, however, expect radically different things. They like the idea of open flowing spaces where they can code for an hour and slide over to play games on a play station for the next hour. The number of choices of tea would be more than the number of programming languages known. A swing chair or a nap pod would be an ideal place to take a break. Companies have to cater to both the ends of the spectrum and create spaces where everyone can engage with their environment and be the most productive.

Driving a car is also about how engaged you are with the environment around you. In India, you need to constantly engage with fellow drivers, pedestrians, street hawkers, dogs, and cows. When I started driving in the US, I had a hard time convincing my senses to get used to the American environment. Sitting on the wrong side of the car I had to constantly tell my right hand to look for the gear lever rather than my left hand. I had to keep my left hand constantly on the steering and not extend to look for the gear lever on the left. This caused a lot of confusion and a few hilarious moments. I did wonder if America switched sides just to get away from the British system.

Even in the case of Lucia, active engagement was being used to make this a crowdsourced and crowdfunded movie and creating brand recall. The updates sent by Pawan were regular and frequent. It's not every day that a common man makes a movie and I was sure that the other folks who pooled in money were also waiting for each update with equal excitement. His mails would arrive in the middle of the nights for me. I would read the updates about the movie and sleep peacefully.

One mail update had a detail which illustrates engagement with the environment.

Some theaters in India are known to play movies which are intended for mature audiences only. There is a stationery store close to one such theater on the Old Airport Road in Bangalore. Whenever my friend and I went to this store we would surreptitiously look at the posters to see what movie was playing at this theater. The movies that played here had names like 'Buffy the vampire lay-er', 'Humpback of Notre dame', 'The Da Vinci Load' and I hope you get the drift. Given the display of explicit posters and its unclean surroundings, many would feel shy to even walk past this theater. The mail that Pawan sent had mentioned that there was a theater in which they were shooting the movie and it was located on the Old Airport Road. There are not many theaters on that road and I was intrigued. He said that the shoot was stalled at this place as the owner, an old man demanded them to stop everything and vacate the place. I wrote to Pawan asking if it was the same theater that I was thinking about and he confirmed back to me in the affirmative. I thought I could help out. This theater belonged to my friend's grandfather. He had leased the place out to someone who was running the place and churning out revenue to the owners. By contacting my friend and making a case for Lucia, I was sure I could restore order and obtain permission to complete the shoot. Before I could get in touch with my friend, I learnt that the owner had allowed the shoot to proceed because of the contractual legalities involved. It's very interesting to understand why the theater management had issues with the film shoot. It is to be noted that the movie shows were not halted at this theatre during the film shoot. There were good looking girls coming in for the shoot while in the projector room a constant flow of explicit material was let loose on the waiting audience down in the hall. The Lucia shoot only brought in additional revenue for the hall owners and did not impact their regular business at all. An Ivy-league business graduate will most likely not be able to guess the root cause of the theater owner's discontentment. The patrons of the movie theater expected dingy surroundings, unkempt hallways, stained walls, and unclean floor. The audience was conditioned to expect a certain kind of environment. The Lucia crew had to shoot scenes where the theater underwent a 180-degree transformation. This meant a complete cleanup of the place and making the place look visually appealing. The crew did not consider that the theater management did not find this appealing at all since it was influencing the patrons to stay away. The management, therefore, declined any permission to clean up the place. After some stand-off, the management and the movie crew had to come to an agreement that the crew would clean up the place, complete their shooting and then mess it all up to make it look as dingy as it was before. Thus, a truce was called and shooting resumed. We had a few more scenes to shoot. Lights, Camera, Action!

Chapter Six: A Dip in the Thames

"Hutsidda devaru, hullu meyisadirutthaneye?" – Kannada Proverb

"Will the god who brought us to the world let us go hungry?"

"Thank you, British Council for two counts, one calling me 'Young' and another giving me this award".

Standing at the podium Pawan spoke about how the award from the British Council added credibility to the movement he had undertaken. Pawan had been recognized as a Creative Young Entrepreneur and was awarded the first prize at a competition. He was humble enough to remember us, the crowd funders, in his acceptance speech. It was an award for his skills and his dedication to the project. The work was still in progress but the efforts of the director had garnered the project an award even before the movie was made. This was probably one of the first times in the Kannada film industry that the British Council bestowed an award to a Kannada (regional language) filmmaker for his trade. Why does an award help ratify or validate something? The movie was not made but the process of making the movie was awarded and that was huge. That boosted the confidence of the team and helped them get visibility on the internet. It brought a global focus on the Kannada film industry.

On Aug 22, 2012, I received an email at around 2 am local time. It felt good to unlock the phone and see Pawan's mail in the inbox. I got a sense of "Your money working for you" when I read that sixty percent of the movie was complete. The movie was at a crucial juncture where there was a decision pending on the ending of the movie which would make this movie either a cult classic or a regular money grosser. Pawan was asking our opinion because he felt that a diversity of opinion was better than one person. I did not know how the others would opine but I instinctively felt that most of them would prefer the movie to be a cult classic. I would like to present another cult classic movie in Kannada which was titled with only the letter "A". The movies in Kannada typically have a tag line associated with it which is a brief about the movie to influence the audience into watching it. The movie 'A' had a creative title and an even more creative tag line which said: "Buddivantarige Maatra" that translates to "For the intelligent only". No person would undermine their intelligence and say the movie was not for them. The movie made good business. There were exceptions to every rule. My friends and I had met up a little after the movie released and one of them asked everyone "Hey guys have you watched the movie 'A'?". "No dude," says one of my friends in a display of rare honesty, "the movie said it was just for the intelligent, so I didn't watch."

I wanted Pawan to be unique and creative in the handling of the subject similar to how 'A' did in most of its aspects. I decided to raise the creativity a notch. I waxed eloquent in my reply to him about why the ending should not tread the beaten track and have one climax. It could have two endings and let the audience decide what ending they would prefer to takeaway. I was neither sure if my response had reached Pawan nor whether it made sense to the script but I was happy to voice my opinion. You must remember that during the entire time the script was kept a secret.

Pawan, in the meanwhile, was planning a trip to London to conduct a film making workshop. Creative folks have their creative means to get funding for such trips and that is how Pawan managed to do this. He was doing his bit in getting the word out there about Lucia on the global stage. I also presented a suggestion to Pawan to do small behind-the-scenes kind of documentary on the auditions and showcase how simple people became film personalities because of Lucia. It could be aired on prime-time television to generate revenue. This idea was included in one of the options presented to a TV channel but for some reason, the economics couldn't be been worked out. I am sure other contributors also wondered why Pawan was taking a break from actually making the movie and going to London for a Film making workshop. But it did not matter once Pawan completed his London trip and returned and plunged straight into film making.

Pawan gave each of us contributors a task to create a small video holding a plaque with our name written on it. The idea was that all the videos would be finally stitched together to create a logo for Audience Films. Yes, we had decided our movement would be called Audience Films. The brief was simple, find a good background with ample light and shoot a small video with a good camera. What happens when you give a software guy a task and a deadline? There is a timer in each of us to not start a task until T-1. The last day is when most of the work gets done just like how all exam preparations happened on the last day. All the crowdfunding do-gooders were excited about the prospect of having a small video of themselves in the larger video.

Chapter Seven: One Chance Please

"Hallidavanige kadale illa. Kadale iddavanige hallilla" – Kannada Proverb

"One who has Teeth does not have peanuts. One who has peanuts has no teeth"

It is not easy to get a break in any profession. In the year 2000, the year I graduated, we did not have campus interviews in our college. This meant we would have to knock on the doors of every company looking for available jobs. This was before online job portals caught on and we relied on the "Ascent" supplement which came along with Wednesday's edition of the Times of India in Bangalore. The thickness of the supplement or the number of pages in Ascent showed how well the Macroeconomy was doing. In the early 2000s, the supplement was more like a magazine. One Wednesday my entire gang of friends and I went for a walk-in selection at an IT company on Lavelle Road. Due to the sheer number of people who walk-in, companies have a multi-step approach to cut through the crowd and arrive at a prospective employee list. That day the first step was a test on aptitude and after the test, we all waited on the terrace helping ourselves to the free fountain soda machine. What more could fresh graduates with very little money in their wallets want! The HR lady came in with the list of candidates who had passed the test. My friends and I were rooting for the most intelligent people in our gang to get selected and I did not feature in that list. But to my surprise, I featured on the list that the HR lady called out. That sent my friends into a tizzy and they cheered for me with gusto. Somewhere on the same terrace, two girls were looking at us bemused. One of them didn't know that she had just seen her soulmate.

Getting into the film industry as a playback singer or musician is a fortune favouring the few. Lucia being a crowdsourced movie wanted to crowdsource singers as well. The trend in those days was to import singers from the Hindi film industry who would render their great voices to Kannada songs without understanding the essence of the song. This had worked in the past and many songs had become outrageous hits. We were going away from the trend and the audition process was also a paradigm shift. Poornachandra Tejaswi, the music director recorded a song in his voice and released it on popular social platforms inviting singers to render the same song in their voices and send back the recordings. The singer they found to be most suited for the song would become the actual playback singer for that song in the movie. The song was a foot-tapping number from Lucia.

Music penetrates your soul, mind, and body like nothing else. Legends say that the raaga Megha Malhar has the power to do cloud seeding. But I am not an expert on this subject so I will not take any more questions on the authenticity of the claim, albeit the water tanker lobby might start looking for the one who can sing this raaga. Right from the time, the music director released this song online for an audition, many of us felt that he had sung it best and none of the submissions could compare. Finally, we took a unanimous decision that he would sing that song even in the movie! The demo track went viral.

Poornachandra Tejaswi composed another foot-tapping folksy number and he wanted an experienced nuanced singer for the same. Poornachandra started the hunt in Mysore and got as far as Mandya before he found the voice for his composition. As kids, we are always asked what we would want to become when we grow up. My kindergartener kid wants to be a king because he firmly believes that when he is the king nobody will tell him what to do. The singer that the music director had found wanted to grow up and be an orchestra singer and he was living his childhood dream spreading joy. Naveen Sajju belonged to a small village called Ballekere. He was the lead singer in a small-town orchestra troupe. Clad in a blazer and clean-shaven he would belt out popular Kannada movie songs from 7 pm to 12 am at different venues. When he was onstage nothing mattered to him other than the songs and the passion showed. The crowds loved him and he always got requests from the crowd to sing their favourite songs. He would sing songs of stars like Dr.Raj Kumar, Mandya's very own Ambareesh, and Shankar Nag among others. All auto drivers at the venue would garland Naveen with garlands made out of currency notes when he would sing a song from Shankar's movies. There is a backstory to this which is a trivia for anyone who lives in Bangalore and wondered why most auto rickshaw stands bear Shankar Nag's name. He made a movie called "Auto Raja" in 1980 in which he was the protagonist and an auto driver despite being a science graduate. Being educated, he offers his riders newspapers to read on the commute. In the movie, he fights criminals, infuses pride in the profession, and shows the way for the auto driver community to have each other's back.

Our music director and movie director felt that Naveen had the perfect earthy voice to sing the folk number in the movie. Stage performers including orchestra singers draw their energy from the audience and perform better with every round of applause. They feel at home staring into the bright lights and singing like there is no tomorrow and dancing like nobody is watching. But if you ask them to sing into a microphone in an empty room, they may not be the same person. Naveen was brought to one such recording studio where he was made to sing one of the songs. He felt like a fish out of water and the onstage energy was completely missing. Poornachandra trained him in an interesting way to get him ready for the song. To improve his diction, he would make him read a Kannada newspaper aloud every day. He also trained him on the dialect required for the song. The rigor of training overwhelmed Naveen and he disappeared one day not to be found. Both Poornachandra and Pawan were baffled that the opportunity to sing in a movie was not enough to motivate an orchestra singer. They took a scientific approach to the training but perhaps did not heed to the emotional signals. They somehow managed to track Naveen down and brought him straight to the recording room and got the song recorded. The result of this experiment was the hit song "Jamma Jamma Ja". Naveen was very pleased when the director asked him to sing it in his next orchestra outing. The makers got the validation they were looking for when the entire audience was on their feet dancing to the song. The songs from Lucia were a raging hit with increasing viewership. More songs were added to the album to make it a complete music album ready for release. Getting the songs ready was the first step in getting closer to revenue generation in this movie.

I have explained the process of zeroing in on the singer and completing the song in a couple of paragraphs. In reality, this process took a whole six months. None of the crew members were being paid much during that time. The credit of managing the shoot related payments and motivating his crew goes to the efficient management of Pawan. By now he had executed the movie shoot in approximately 30 lakhs. It might sound plausible but in reality, it was due to the generosities of various people involved. Many worked for the movie and had deferred receiving their compensation. A few people to name are Badal Nanjundaswamy and Shashidhar Adapa for art, Vydurya as a Stylist, Ashok for locations. Small humane acts can come together to build a product or a happy life.

A few years back, when my daughter was 9 months old, we decided to get her ears pierced. To a parent seeing their child cry is normal. Most kids cry. But when the kids cry due to an action of the parent it hurts the most. A vaccine prick is one thing but putting a hole through her ears was a different ball game. We lured her into a joy ride and felt very guilty when she happily agreed. At the jeweler's store, she was amazed by all the lights and did not seem to pay much attention when her mom held her a little too tightly. Soon the joy on her face disappeared and there was a look of despair in her eyes. She looked at me with big tears coming out of those big trusting eyes and I felt ashamed for taking pictures. Her mom bundled her up in her arms and took her out onto the street to distract her. She was still crying when an aged fruit vendor offered a small banana to the crying child. My daughter dislikes strangers but her eyes lit up to see this woman and she happily accepted the banana and ate it all up. She had stopped crying. This whole episode lasted for about four minutes but it seemed like a lifetime to us. We thanked the divine intervention and I expressed my gratitude by buying a sufficient quantity of fruit from the lady. They say it takes a village to raise a child. Similarly, Lucia was very much being raised by an entire community!

There were innumerable technicians, staff, musicians, singers, art team, cameramen, and others whose generosity with regards to taking pay cuts or deferring them to a later date were the main reasons this movie got made. The entire shoot of the movie was completed in 65 days. On Jun 10th the Audio Release of Lucia was announced on Social Media. We had a buyer Anand Audio who paid for the songs and also got corporate sponsors from 'Lenovo' and 'Taxi for Sure'. For the corporate sponsors, we had product placement to help their product gain visibility through the songs. Ananya Bhat, Udith Haritas, Naveen Sajju, Bappi Blossom, Monish Kumar, and Poornachandra performed the songs live. One of the songs became my 5-year-old daughter's favourite. On long road trips, our car was filled with "Nee Thoreda Galigeyali" rendered from the car stereo and by the happy back seat occupant. Unknowingly singers touch the lives of many but many remain unknown.

Chapter Eight: Bond with the Best

"Hottege Hittu illa, juttige mallige hu" – Kannada Proverb

"No food to eat but adorning hair with jasmine flowers"

Lucia was invited to submit its entry to the London Indian Film Festival. The thought itself was exhilarating. What started as a crowdsourced experiment had now reached a stage where we might have the first showing of the movie in London. We felt that maybe the UK based investors would get to watch the movie first. Pawan got in touch with the London based investors and some of the operational issues were sorted by them. Pawan and the DOP Siddharth got to travel to London to participate in the Festival which would be a contest of sorts. Crowdfunding helped this visit as well since Pawan got to stay with the first contributor for Lucia, Madhusudan.

We were competing against some of the best movies. The featured opening was by 'Monsoon Shootout' starring Nawazuddin Siddiqui. This movie had already garnered high interest at the Cannes film festival. There was also the omnibus Directorial, 'Bombay Talkies' which had an ensemble of Directors from Hindi like Karan Johar, Anurag Kashyap, Zoya Aktar and Dibakar Banerjee. A Marathi feature film Pune 52, Hindi/Punjabi movie BA Pass, Oriya feature film Oonga, starring Nandita Das, Life is Good starring Jackie Shroff, and Adoor Gopalkrishnan's Elippathayam a Malayalam movie and a few other movies which were competing with our own Lucia. The day of the event was approaching and it was a sellout. July 18th, 2013 would be the first show of Lucia in London. This would be the second Kannada movie to be part of this film festival in London and the first mainstream movie to have its premiere in London. Lucia sold the highest number of tickets at the festival. The brief given to all those who were to watch the movie was to maintain complete secrecy about the storyline since it had not yet had a theatrical release. Murphy's law reared its head again at the screening in

London. Technology has a great way to show that it still rules. Something that was working fine would just stop working.

This has happened so many times to me. I would write a piece of code and test it many times. After reaching a level of confidence that it would work when the boss is trying it out, I would take it to the boss and have him try it. When the boss would get at my desk to review it, the code would never work in spite of trying umpteen times. As soon as he would leave it would start working. Something similar happened to the Lucia team at the London Indian Film Festival.

They had the movie in digital format. But the format was not supported at the theater that they planned to screen it on. It was a task now to convert into the right format and ensure it played. That would take time as any video conversion is not a simple matter. The last resort used was to quit trying to convert the video into the required format but plug in the laptop to the projector and have the audience watch the movie!

This was the first time someone was watching our movie. Not everyone in the cast had seen the completed movie. Eighteen months of effort that went into making the movie was seeing the light of day. The audience that watched the movie gave a standing ovation to the team. This was a dream result for all the investors who had invested and bought tickets to a movie that was not yet made. Their faith had paid off and I was immensely happy that the audience who watched the show gave very positive reviews of the movie. The story was not yet done, "picture abhi baaki hain mere dost". London was not yet done. We were pleasantly surprised when a mail from Pawan informed us about the victory of our movie against the other movies at the Film Festival. Lucia had managed to win the Audience Choice Awards at LIFF 2013. Lucia was the best movie that the audience liked! It took some time for this to sink in our minds. The news that this movie won an award was to be announced by none other than Irrfan Khan, the Bollywood/Hollywood actor! He wanted to watch the movie after hearing the buzz and seeing that the audience liked it. Pawan scheduled a private screening for Irrfan at his residence and he helped the team by putting out a short video about the movie. That, till date, was the most generous act by a bonafide star for the movie. He did not charge any money for the same. He did it out of his goodwill. This helped to get the required attention from the mainstream folks as well.

We believed that this would open up the gates for us to release the movie commercially to a wide audience back home in India. We were very positive about this. On the contrary, something else was in store for us back home. At the start of this book, I had written about how an "award" movie is received in India. Something similar happened to Lucia. The South Indian Film Industry has four big players. Telugu, Tamil, Malayalam, and Kannada. Most movies bank on the Satellite rights that gives Television Channels exclusive rights to telecast the movie. At this point, a Tamil movie with an unknown cast got an offer of 1.7 Crores for its satellite rights. Our movie got an offer which was nowhere close to this. The audio was a huge hit, there was a huge buzz around the movie in the social media circles and it had a unique crowd support. Still, we did not get the valuation we demanded. One of the reasons was that our movie was now getting classified as an award movie which will be artsier rather than appeal to the masses. It looked like the Television channels were not willing to take the risk.

We had another problem to solve at this point. Even before the release was planned the pirates of the movie industry were readying up their side of the story to get content out there. Search Engine Optimization is a technology that enables your page rank to be higher compared to other search results. How does one achieve this? There are numerous ways to do that. Even before the movie was complete the pirates had put up their websites to ensure traffic flows to their site once the movie was available. Pawan had an idea to thwart this as much as possible. The best way was to create more such clones which will ensure legal sites to be more visible than the pirated sites. If a blog is created with the information about Lucia the page rank would include that as well in the search result. If more people did this then it would make it less easy for people to find the pirated sites.

The general public had an opportunity here. Pawan had opened up a new way to distribute movies. In the movie-making process, producing the movie is just half the job. Post-production is a mammoth effort to get it in front of the paying customer. There is a big component called Distribution. Distributors purchase the rights of screening the movie in the cinema halls for a fee. They can decide how well the movie does. What Pawan did for Lucia was a little different. There was a partnership with an online content delivery platform called Distrify. One could purchase the right to be a distributor of the movie online. This is a little different from being an Amway salesperson or any other multi-level marketing campaign one has heard of.

I was at a wedding and there was this guy who I had never seen before approach me. He started with his question of what I was doing and where I worked. His next question threw me out of gear. He wanted to come home and talk with me. I didn't know why he wanted to do that but I couldn't refuse as he was a distant relative and I was seeing him for the first time in my life. Anyway, I did oblige and he did come home. His first question was what my favorite car was, the next question favorite holiday destination. I stopped him at that point and asked him if he was trying to sell me some Amway product. He was a little offended at my question but he agreed that he was trying to do that. I asked him to end his sales pitch and to finish his coffee and leave. I had no intention of becoming an Amway sales guy.

Now at this point, we had the opportunity to become marketing agents for Lucia. This idea although seemed great but I had my doubts about this working very well. Both Siri and I had been talking about Lucia on social media and how it was an honest attempt. Many people might have blocked us because of our 'Lucia rants'. Despite that, we went ahead with the plan. The plan was to purchase the online distribution rights of Lucia by paying an advance pre-order. With this, one would get a link that was personalized. Now the next task was to provide this link to friends and family who wanted to watch the movie online. The catch was if they purchased using the provided customized link, we would get a percentage share in the revenue. Now we got our link and we went ahead and shared it with our friends and family. This was to be used post the online distribution began. How much money did we make from this channel? You'll find out soon. Using this technique, the movie had close to 1300 online distributors. This brought in close to 18 lakh INR revenue for the movie.

Chapter Nine: Silver Screen

"Kallanigondu pille nepa" – Kannada Proverb

"A Thief needs a small excuse for his theft"

Do you know why the big screen is known as the "Silver Screen" in the cinema industry? To give you a piece of trivia, it is because in the early years of motion picture industry actual silver or reflective aluminum content was embedded in the material that made up the screen's highly reflective surface. I came to know of this from Wikipedia, the one who knows everything.

To show a movie on the silver screen, the moviemakers have to get a certificate from the censor board which is the rating authority. This would allow the theatres and other platforms to ensure that the movie is reaching the right audience. Censor boards work differently in different countries. Siri and I, like so many parents of young kids, are constantly worried about what will be shown on TV in the next scene of a movie or the advertisements. There have been instances where watching a cricket match on television has led to embarrassing moments during the advertisement breaks. In the summer of 2013, a Hindi movie about a very famous athlete released in the local theaters. Wanting to make an impression of trying hard and succeeding, we took our 5-year-old daughter to watch it in the theatre. A few minutes into the movie we realized that it was not a kid-friendly movie in the theaters in the US.

Siri wanted to know what kind of rating Lucia would get. It would be very difficult to tell people about the movie if it was for mature audiences only. But fears came to rest soon.

Lucia got a rating of 'U' in India which stood for Universal. Which meant it was view worthy across all ages. The director had to remove a couple of swear words to reach that milestone. I was glad about this and informed Siri who was elated! Technically, we could ask our daughter to watch this movie and also look forward to the fact that she might be proud of it one day!

One fine day we got an email from Pawan. We had waited 18 months for this email. The subject of the mail was 'ur premier pass', All in small letters. The pass was exclusively for people in, well, Bangalore.

The most unforgettable cricket match for a Bangalorean, before IPL, is the one that was played at Chinnaswamy Stadium. It was a world cup quarter-final match between India and Pakistan in 1996. It was the 14th over and Pakistan was doing well. Amir Sohail was the batsman and Venkatesh Prasad was the bowler. Sohail had just completed getting fifty runs and was facing Venkatesh Prasad. Amir hit a ball to the boundary for four runs and acted like he had won the world cup! He signaled to Prasad indicating that the next ball would be dispatched there as well and he needed to pack up! Undaunted, what Prasad did next was to send Sohail packing into the stands! The audacity of Sohail was that he waved his bat at the fans while he walked out despite being booed by the spectators. This match has been etched in my memory since this was a day before an important exam. As luck would have it we had managed to get one ticket for this match. Due to my exams, I could not go and my brother got to see the live-action of this match.

We were in Kansas and were reading the email from Pawan. Siri and I had a mix of emotions. We were filled with happiness at the premier and unhappy at not being able to attend it. We even wondered whether we would ever get a chance to watch the movie on the big screen! I forwarded the mail from Pawan to my brother who was more than happy to attend the Premiere show! The movie premiere was held in Cinepolis Bangalore on 5th September 2013.

I missed being there on day 1 when the movie premiered. My brother, Sunil, called me after the show to tell us that he loved the movie. He was thrilled to see my name on the big screen as an Associate Producer. My sister in law who had accompanied him also complimented us and made us feel special. They had only good things to tell us about the premier. Sunil gave us a lot of details just like the highlights of a cricket match. Siri and I were a tad bit sad that although we had funded the movie there was no way for us to watch the movie. At the same time happy that the ensuing reviews were great and people liked the end product. We slept well that night.

The film was released pan India on the 6th of Sep. India-wide release for a crowdfunded Kannada movie was a big deal in itself but to be released as PVR Director's Rare was a unique distinction. The movie shows in Karnataka were running packed. We got an update from Pawan about the collections, which was indeed great. The hope was that the movie would run for at least four weeks in cinema halls. The day that all the cast and crew were waiting for was here and it was a big relief that the reviews were very good as well. My cousins tagged me on a popular social media platform that they were watching Lucia in cinema halls. They said the entire gang whistled and whooped on seeing my name in the "Associate Producers" list in the title card. This was a 'never before and maybe never after' moment for me.

The list of theaters outside of Karnataka where the movie released is as below.

PVR Juhu Mumbai
PVR Phoenix Lower Parel Mumbai
PVR Goregaon Mumbai
PVR Mulund Mumbai
PVR ECX Andheri Mumbai
PVR Kurla Mumbai
Cinemax Versova Mumbai

PVR MGF Mall Gurgaon
PVR Naraina Delhi
PVR Phoenix Marketcity Pune
PVR Ampa Skywalk Chennai
PVR Lulu Mall Cochin
PVR Acropolis Mall Ahmedabad
PVR Rahul Raj Mall Surat

Cinemax Cyberabad (Hyderabad)

Cinepolis - Bhopal, Surat and Ahmedabad

Media reports claimed the movie to be a "box office hit". It was a successful experiment that went on to make money. We got a detailed debrief on the financials. By the end of two weeks, the movie had made Twice the budget of the movie. Of this 50% would come to the movie makers. The rest would go to the Theater owners for renting their premises. Second-week earnings for the producers was close to 70% of the movie budget after deductions from the theater rentals. We got information that before the theatrical release the satellite rights of the movie were sold for a decent sum of money. Although this could have been higher compared to other movies given the parameters that this movie had it was a decent amount. The decision on the distribution of remake rights revenue was again handled democratically through voting. Three options were presented with the first being that it would lie entirely with the producers, second that it would be with the creator (Pawan and team), and thirdly it would be shared equally by the two parties. The results of the vote were that it should be split equally between the two parties.

At this juncture, I should talk about the distribution option I had purchased. The number of people who bought the viewing access using the link that I shared was very small, so small that it is embarrassing to quantify. There were many inquiries from friends and relatives about the link and the process to purchase online but it did not convert to sales. I am sure I was not alone in this frustration of getting people to buy. Something that Pawan wrote to us cemented this belief. He wrote that he had met a stranger in Mumbai who recognized Pawan and gave him Rs.500. The stranger explained that he had watched Lucia after downloading from torrent and felt guilty and he thought by paying the director for the ticket money would redeem him. By the time the movie was released and at the time of compiling these statistics, 65000 illegal attempts had been made to pirate Lucia. This would be the work of people who could afford laptops, high-speed internet connections, were most likely educated, and had a job. These are 65000 affluent people who were trying to take away from the honest and hard work of the crew. The 110 people who invested lost out on that opportunity to make money which technically belonged to them. Many people want to watch

Kannada movies either at home on a DVD or some television channel for free. If the 65,000 illegal accesses are converted into real revenue that would have made a real big difference. If the price was 10 USD per view that is converted to 3.9 Crore in Indian Rupees considering an exchange rate of 60 Rs per dollar! Even if we discount 75%, 1 Crore was still a huge revenue for the Kannada film industry back in 2013.

People are spread across the world and some of them want to watch good quality content without paying for it and some spoof their IP location to access torrents. One user on twitter boasted about how he was able to get the DVD rip of Lucia and he wanted to now send it to his girlfriend!

I hope I have successfully illustrated that a movie's fate is quite literally in the hands of the audience. The audience can do as they please but when an honest attempt is made the community needs to step up and do their bit and retain their trust. That will help the movie, makers, and the industry to prosper. The next director, actor, singer, cameraman might be from amidst the audience. Everyone must pay it forward.

Amidst all this, I got an opportunity to travel to India from Kansas in September 2013. My mom decided to return to India after her vacation in the US and I hopped on the same flight for more than one reason! Lucia was still running in theatres and I would have the opportunity to watch Lucia on the big screen. This was bigger than anything else in my list of things to do in Bangalore which included eating breakfast at Brahmin's coffee bar and 'Masala Dose' at CTR.

On Sep 15th, 2013 I got a chance to watch Lucia. What started nearly a year and a half ago ended on that day when I watched Lucia. The songs had been my child's anthem for the past few months and I had to control myself from erupting into an impromptu jig. I was emotional seeing all the details of the movie which we had discussed over emails and they had all turned out like how I had imagined. It felt great to see my name appear on the big 70 mm screen. Not sure if it will ever happen again but I was happy to exult in the moment. I updated the

About Me sections of my social presence as "Associate Producer – Audience Films".

Chapter Ten: Red Carpet

"Kai Kesaraadre baayi mosaru" – Kannada Proverb

"The person who works hard never goes hungry"

This world is for smart people like Sharath. He built a well-designed web site and invested in Search Engine Optimization. He spent time and energy in his planning phase. When the movie was available for online views, he purchased the online distribution rights for Lucia at a 50% return option. What this meant was he would get 50% of all the sales made from his website. He made the best return on investment from the online distribution channel. He invested Rs.2500 to procure distribution rights plus some more for the website itself and in return made 1.8 Lakh INR from sales! I believe the ingenuity of Lucia brought many creative geniuses to the fore.

Before we knew it, the movie had crossed the 50th day of the theatrical show and there was a big party to celebrate the same. All the cast and crew and the crowd contributors, at least those who were fortunate to be in Bangalore, were part of this. Over the next few days, it was clear that the movie had done its run in the theaters and it would cost us more to keep it in the cinema halls. 19th Dec 2013, which marked the 100th day of the movie, was also going to be the last show for the movie. A dream run had come to an end, an ending that nobody expected but everyone was extremely proud of, it was a good closure for the entire team.

There were many personal wins with this movie. It had given a new direction in life for many of us. There was a note of thanks from the mother of Naveen the singer. Holding his payment cheque in her hand, with tears of joy in her eyes she recounted how the entire village had ridiculed her for not sending Naveen to the city for his studies. Instead, he had pursued his passion to be an Orchestra singer which had led to him becoming a playback singer in the movies.

She was overjoyed and would now mark her life as "Before Lucia" and "After Lucia".

Not only Naveen's but the entire team's payments were settled by the movie maker. The folks, like me, who contributed to the movie got returns equal to nearly twice their investments. Considering two years of investment for an Associate Producer the CAGR would be close to 34%, adding the remake rights earnings as well it would work out to nearly 41%. This was a great return on investment. Refer to the table below for other details.

Investment	CAGR
25,000	34.16
50,000	34.16
2,50,000	34.16

Lucia, the movie, chartered new territory, gathered numerous accolades, and brought a plethora of opportunities for the cast and crew. Some of the recognition garnered are:

1) First Kannada Movie to be Crowdfunded and Crowdsourced.

2) First Kannada Movie with a World Premiere in London.

3) First Kannada Film to win the best film award in LIFF.

4) First Kannada Film to come out on Blu-Ray.

5) First Kannada film in 75 years to have an all India release on the same day.

6) Filmfare south, Best director Pawan for Lucia.

7) Filmfare Best supporting actor, Achyuta Kumar for Lucia.

8) Filmfare Best singer male Poornachandra Tejaswi for Lucia.

9) Karnataka State Award for Best music director for Lucia.

10) First Kannada movie to have an English book.

11) First Kannada feature film to be shot completely using a Canon 5D camera.

12) Mirchi award (2014) - Poornachandra Tejaswi - Upcoming Music Composer for Lucia.

13) Big FM Award (2014) - Poornachandra Tejaswi - Best Debut song for Lucia.

14) Karnataka State Award 2013 for Best Singer Naveen Sajju, Lucia.

When I visited India in Nov 2013, I took an auto-rickshaw from Old Airport Road to Basavanagudi to visit my father-in-law. Typically, this is not my preferred means of transport but since I was in India for a short while, I did not have a vehicle of my own. The auto driver was in a happy mood and had the radio tuned to a Kannada station. Right after we crossed Domlur a song started playing on the radio and he saw me getting interested in the song. He asked me if I had watched "Lucia". That piqued my curiosity and I responded in the negative to gauge his reaction. He turned all the way around to look me in the face and tell me to drop all other plans and go watch the movie that very day. He went further and told me that the movie was exceptionally good and he had "sakkath maja" watching it. His favorite song was the one that was playing on the radio "Thin beda kami nee nanna thaleya". We began to sing it together.

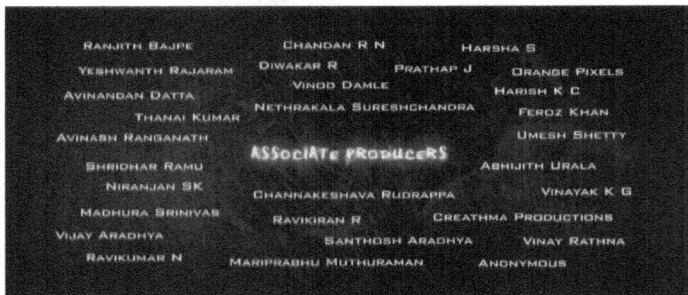

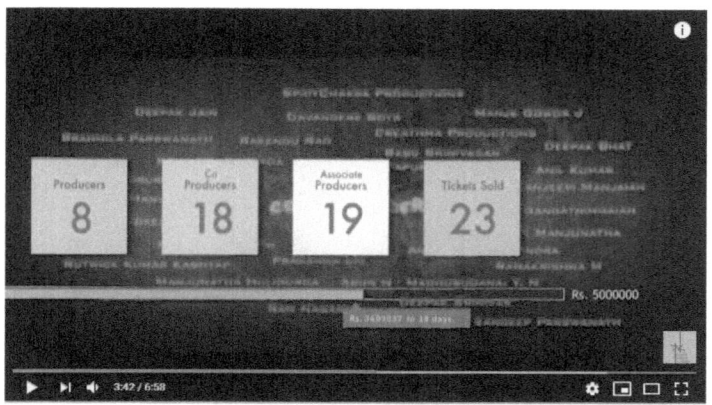

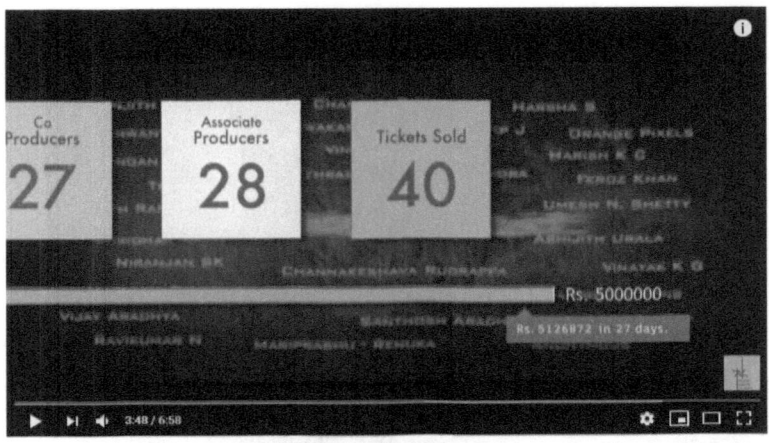

"Sir, koi acchi movie hai to bataon. Lockdown main saare movies dekhliya."

"Arre Lucia dekhi hain? Kannada movie hain."

"Nahin dekhi hain. Accha hain kya?"

"Dekh lo, crowdsourced movie hain. I am one of the crowd that supported the making of the movie."

"Arre wah. Acchi baat hain. Ruko dekhta hun milega ki nahin. Mujhe subtitles wali chahiyen"

"SunNxt pe hain lekin subtitles nahin hain. Lock down hain warna mere paas Blu-Ray bhi padi hain".

"Arre sir, Torrent pe hain. With subtitles, Blu-Ray print. Dekh lun?"

Epilogue

This book is about people. People who got their dreams fulfilled through this one major event in their life called Lucia. You might be wondering what happened to all these people after Lucia but I can tell you about a few of them.

Poornachandra Tejaswi

Poornachandra today has close to 14 movies under his belt post, Lucia. He is one of the leading music directors in the Kannada Film Industry and is sought after for his style in music. He has no regrets leaving behind the Tech Industry that he was part of before Lucia. Working with twelve directors other than Pawan, he wishes that there were more than 24 hours in a day!

Sathish Ninasam

Lucia was not the first movie for Sathish but it allowed him to be a lead actor for the first time. After Lucia, he has been starring as the lead in many movies. He has close to 16 movies to his credit and the number keeps increasing. He went on to win the Filmfare critics award for the movie Ayogya. With Lucia, he was able to show to the world that he could carry a movie on his shoulders.

Sruthi Hariharan

Sruthi started her acting career in Malayalam but Lucia became her foray into Kannada and the opportunity to star as a lead actor. After Lucia, she went on the act in many movies across different languages and even won the State Film Award for Best Actress for the movie Beautiful Manasugalu. In 2018 she acted in Nathicharami for which she won the National Award – Special Mention Best Actress ost of other awards.

Naveen Sajju

The wild card entry into Lucia, Naveen, has cemented his place in the Kannada Film Industry. Other than singing for Kannada movies he has also contested in the game show Bigg Boss in its Season 6. He ended up being the runner up of the show. To his credit, he has more than 150 songs in the industry. He might be one of the few singers who has had so many songs but still did not have a Wikipedia entry as of Jun 2020!

Ananya Bhat

Lucia was the platform for Ananya to launch her career in playback singing. Since then she has sung in many languages including all South Indian languages and Hindi. She won the Filmfare best playback singer award in 2017 for the song 'Namma kaayo devane'. Her career has taken a turn towards acting in television shows, theater, and movies.

Udith Haritas

Udith got instant fame with one song in Lucia. He is multi-talented and is an actor, music composer, and singer. He hopes to nurture talent through the recording studio that he plans to set up.

Pawan Kumar

Pawan used to have an email address that had the word "actor" in it. After Lucia, he has changed that, and now it does not have anything to do with "acting". Soon after things are looking brighter for him as he has been getting a lot more acting opportunities! He has gone on to direct a movie called U-Turn. This movie too was a huge hit. It was made in other South Indian languages. He has also started Pawan Kumar Studios to encourage good and quality content in the Kannada Film Industry.

Bibliography

https://en.wikipedia.org/wiki/61st_Filmfare_Awards_South#Kannada_cinema

https://en.wikipedia.org/wiki/Poornachandra_Tejaswi_(composer)

https://en.wikipedia.org/wiki/Ananya_Bhat

https://en.wikipedia.org/wiki/Sathish_Ninasam

https://en.wikipedia.org/wiki/Sruthi_Hariharan

https://www.imdb.com/title/tt2358592/?ref_=fn_al_tt_2

Acknowledgments

I thank my fellow investors who pitched in to make this movie. Here is the complete list of those that crowdfunded Lucia:

Co-Producers	Associate Producers	Producers
Anil kumar	Abhijith Urala	Anurag Ramachandra
Anurag Ramachandra	Anonymous	Biswajith K Setty
Babu Srinivasan	Avinandan Datta	Creathma Productions
Brahmila Parswanath	Avinash Ranganath	Madhusudan Venkata
BVR Manjunath	Chandan R N	Mahesh Lokhande
Chiranjeevi Manjaiah	Channkeshava Rudrappa	Manjunath TC
Creathma Productions	Creathma Productions	Manoj Jaganmurthy
Davangere Boys	Diwakar R	Santhosh Kumar S R
Deepak Bhat	Feroz Khan	Shivaram
Deepak Jain	Harish K C	Sowmya Jaganmurthy
Deepak Srinivas	Harsha S	Suresh Kanchusthambham
Gururaj Shivakumar	Madhura Srinivas	Vibha Kashyap Productions
Kirangiri Sharada	Mariprabhu Muthuraman	
Lokesh Bangera	Nethrakala Sureshchandra	
Madhusudhana YN	Niranjan SK	
Mahesh K Manjunatha	Orange Pixels	
Manje Gowda J	Prathap J	
Manjunatha Hulidurga	Ranjith Bajpe	
Mouli	Ravikiran R	
Prasanna LM	Ravikumar N	
Rakendu Rao	Santhosh Aradhya	
Ram Nagraj	Shridhar Ramu	
Ramakrishna M	Thanai Kumar	
Ranga	Umesh Shetty	
Rutwick Kumar Kashyap	Vijay Aradhya	
Sandeep P	Vinay Rathna	
Sandesh Hanumelingu	Vinayak K G	
Sharath	Vinod Damle	
Spicy Chakra Productions	Yeshwanth Rajaram	
Vinay		

About the Author

Thanai Kumar is one of the Associate Producers of the movie Lucia. He is a true Bangalorean who watches movies in all languages including Kannada. His steadfast belief in creating good movies in the Kannada language led him to crowdfund this movie. He is a long-time blogger and a first-time author.